AF604478

KEEPING IT REAL

-THE JOY OF EVERYDAY LIFE-

By

Longinus Onyechesi

First published in 2016.

Freedom Publishing Books
6 Malvern Street
Bayswater Victoria, Australia 3153

ISBN: 978-0-9925406-2-3

Printed in Australia by Brougham Press
33 Scoresby Road Bayswater 3153

This book is dedicated to

The Cooper family
Michele, Samara, Nathaniel and Shelton

LIFE definitely is our best teacher.
It either teaches us now or later.
As for teaching us, it surely will.

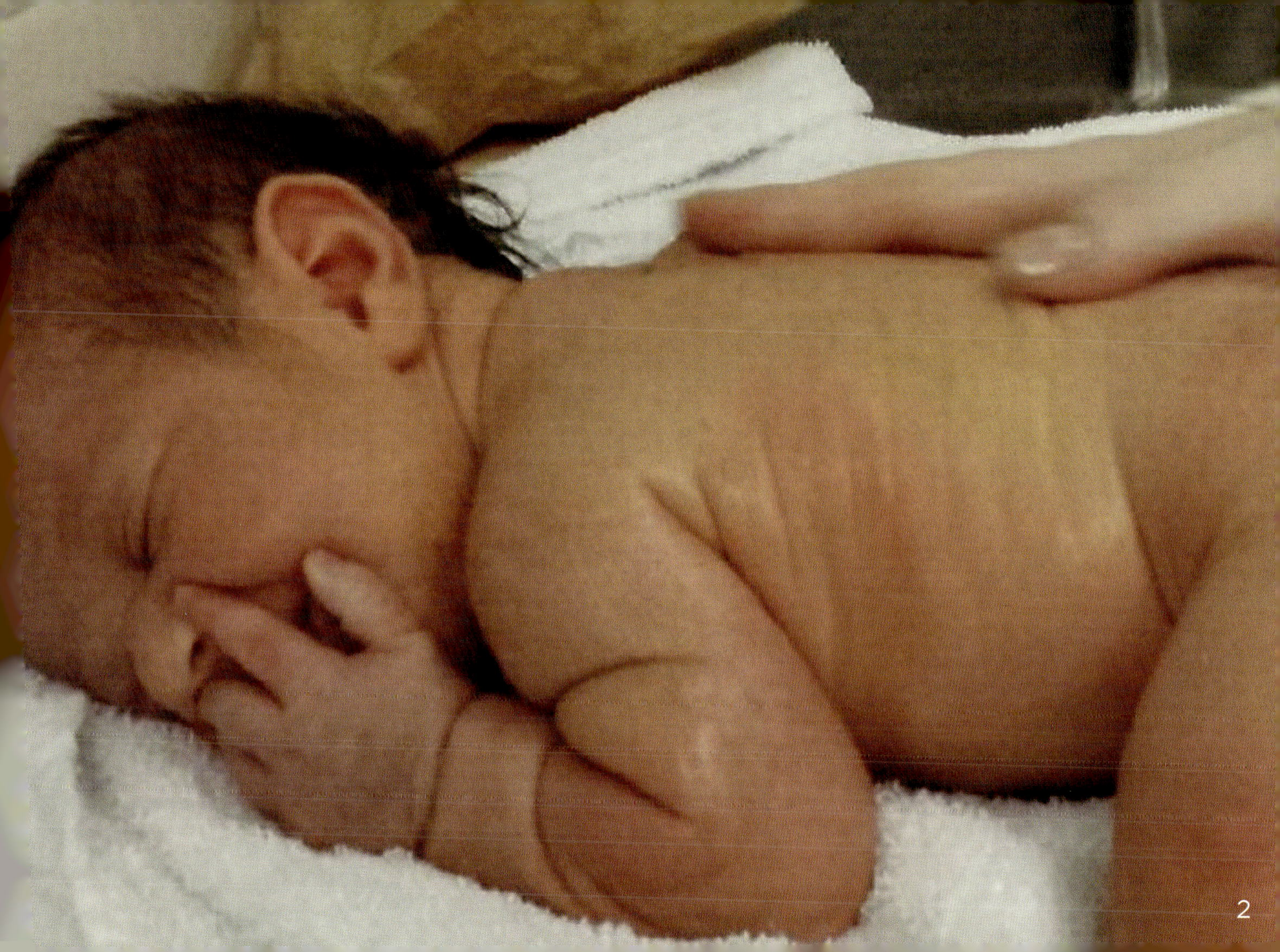

SOME MOMENTS
in life leave us inconsolable
despite the sweetest of words.

Words are often not enough.
Silence sometimes is.

FOCUS
not on what used to be,
for it is no longer.

ACCEPT what is,
for it is what you've got.

BE OPEN to what will be –
life is in constant flux.

THERE comes that moment in our lives when,
despite strength, confidence and seeming successes,
there still feels some sort of emptiness beneath.

IT is not always easy
to share yourself with someone.

It involves lots of struggles.
However, that's what it takes to be in love.

FOCUS less on the inabilities and faults of a friend
so that you may discover and appreciate
the latent riches in his/her abilities and strengths.

TRUE FRIENDS ARE HARD TO FIND.

NEVER mistake someone's meekness for a weakness or take undue advantage of someone's patience. We've all got the beast in us.

Be careful not to unleash it.

When the quest for MIRACLES becomes incessant,
it tends to becloud our God-given abilities
and seduces us into uncalculated beliefs.

The ability to accommodate
differences in individuals
seems the hallmark of
contemporary education and
ENLIGHTENMENT.

Co robi, jakie ma hobby?
Co go cieszy?
Wiek;

Be always as happy as you can and
leave not today's happiness for tomorrow
nor compromise that which makes you
HAPPY.

Do not be ASHAMED
to identify with your inabilities.

For we are all
not yet perfect.

BE careful to not subject the young
to unquestioned obedience.

You may succeed at the moment
but they may end up rebels.

Endeavour to live within existing realities even as you look up to the transcendence.

There seems a big gap between the

IDEAL AND REALITY.

Bother not to go back to the way things were because things will never remain as they were.

ALWAYS, be open to the possibilities of the future.

Though the realities of life may clip
the wings of our dreams and fantasies,
we should always

ENDEAVOUR TO FLY

because dreams keep us sustained.

Who we are matters more than
who we were and who we shall become.

The past exists in our memory.
The future in our imagination.
The present is all we have.

ENJOY EVERY BIT OF IT.

None of us may be easy to live with,
not even the best of FRIENDS.

It takes the enduring patience
of the other to accommodate.

We all could be annoying
at one point or another.

Be open to the opinions of the other, in matters of common interest.

We all approach reality from different backgrounds and

PERSPECTIVES.

Be careful to not think
you know what is best for the other.

Shoes may look the same but fit differently.

Interests and motivations
differ in INDIVIDUAL persons.

SYCOPHANCY never promotes the integrity of any person, neither does it enhance the progress of any group.

POSITIVE criticism, sometimes, seems the most patriotic, but so hard to accommodate.

THE LIFE we live is not a rehearsal, unlike a play
it admits of neither edition nor audition.

Its scripts are written only as they are performed.
Enjoy your part while still on the stage.

THE CLUB DAYS
OF GUNS N' ROSES
SG
Special

Better travel the road of DESTINY
through the vehicle of aspiration
than that of competition.

Everyone runs a particular lane
within their peculiar speed ability.

DESTINY differs.

When religious interpretations and manner of faith communication no longer liberate the SOUL nor enlighten the MIND, religion could become a veritable tool of enslavement.

No one plays for too long
in the game of life.

SO, play with maximized abilities
while still in the game and
have less regrets for losses.

Gestures of acknowledgement and appreciation could serve as lubricants to sustain the efforts and strength of those who care for us.

BECAUSE CARING TAKES ENERGY.

THE LIFE we lead is not
just the effect of our backgrounds,
experiences, choices and interests,
but more of our beliefs.

BELIEFS shape actions.

Though the tides of life
may hit you hard, never give up.

There is always a reason to LIVE.

Although the pain of yesterday may seem to endure,
the hope of tomorrow sustains us the more.

Each day it hurts a little less.

Wounds HEAL with time.

We've all got something BEAUTIFUL
and amazing in each one of us.

It only takes the interest and
positive-mindedness of the other
to be recognised and appreciated.

Sometimes we need to take RISKS
to effect the changes we desire.

Things don't just move,
they are moved.

We all have scripts that are
better kept from the public.

Truly, no one is without shortcomings.

Be MINDFUL while you judge others.

"The right choice is not
always the best choice."

"Break the rules, sometimes,
to free your heart."

- Anonymous -

We can always do BETTER,

Don't give up.

Despite careful and thoughtful checks and balances, there still remain unforeseeable effects of the decisions we make.

We are really LIMITED.

Always give yourself time
to heal whenever you are hurt.

Healing is a process and it takes TIME.

There comes that moment in life
when it seems nobody can
understand your pain.

It really hurts.

Nothing is so painful
as the LOSS of a loved one.

It sometimes takes a painful experience to reveal a person's innate BEAUTY and pathway to DESTINY.

ENDEAVOUR to make peace with existing realities while pursuing your dreams.

Things are not always what they seem.

Only when we could fit into the other's shoes
would we truly understand them.

It is easier to judge people
than to UNDERSTAND them.

Be sure to always
challenge your limitations
and confront your fears if
you want to

KEEP GROWING.

DEFEND
CANADIAN
CANADIAN

To appreciate the DIFFERENCES
in others we must be willing
to challenge our PERCEPTIONS.

THINK
OUTSIDE
THE BOX

POSITIVE changes in life often involve painful experiences.

There can't be any resurrection without death.

Never think you have life all planned.
Each day is full of revelations.
Leave room for what is to come.

Life is a JOURNEY.

What turns you on today
might drive you nuts tomorrow.
So, be careful to not make
inflexible decisions.

Things change with TIME.

BE MINDFUL as you bask in the euphoria
that comes with falling in love.

Love is sustained more
by constant efforts and decisions
than by spontaneous emotions.

It is a great challenge
to sustain intimate relationships
as our EMOTIONS often get in the way.

Our good intents should keep us on track.

We are all on a leash, full of invisible chains.
Some we are able to break from,
others we are stuck to.

No one is entirely FREE.

45

SOMETIMES, we accept things
not because they are the best but
because we cannot change them.

We are all UNIQUE.
No one must be like the other.

There is nothing wrong
in being different.

Be yourself.

There is that WILD side to us
which only the right person can activate.

People impact on us differently.

WE'VE all got our soft spots.
Tune into them, and we
will yield to your whims.

Today's events play a part
in the memories of tomorrow,
because tomorrow is not totally
independent of yesterday.

Make good memories
while you LIVE TODAY.

Do not let the child in you grow old;
else you miss out on a lot of FUN.

The tides of LIFE weaken
our resilience over time.

The older we get the more
susceptible we become.

Some people come into our lives
for a short while leaving an
impression for a life time.

Of such people MEMORY refuses to let go.

Acknowledgement

I acknowledge, in great measures, all who in their respective ways contributed to the success of this work; My parents, brothers and sisters, Rev. Fr. Ian W Ranson, Rob and Mari Mendoza, Jing and Rosa Sosa, Fred and Rita Barbara, Michele Cooper, Shelton Cooper, Nathaniel Cooper, Samara Cooper, Sherry-Rose Watts, Joseph Duong, Dick and Denise Nowakowski, Chimaobi Oyibo, Michelle Penson, Peter Penson, Dr. Chigozie Agbarakwe, Ebere Agbarakwe, Len Regan, Mary White, Damian Murphy, Fr. Brian Collins, Dr Mimmie Ngum-Chi Watts, and Dr. Chris Watts. You are all appreciated.

Experience shows that there is more to the journey of life than we can imagine. **'Keeping It Real'** is a collection of thoughts and experiences expressed in quotes to accompany us on this journey.

It relates with our experiences, challenges our perceptions, inspires our thoughts and motivates our actions to the understanding that despite ideas, predictions and plans, there still remains the unexpected in life.
We keep it real when we acknowledge the past, accommodate the present and open up to the future.

Picture credits

Denise and Dick Nowakowski
2, 10, 22, 24, 28, 34, 64, 76, 88, 98, 102

Longinus, Marie and Michelle
20, 46, 78

www. Pixel. Com
4, 6, 8, 16, 18, 30, 36, 38, 40, 42, 44, 48, 50, 56, 66, 72, 82, 84, 96, 104, 110

Stock photos
12, 14, 26, 32, 52, 54, 58, 60, 62, 68, 70,74, 80, 86, 90, 92, 94, 100, 106, 108, 112

Fr Longinus Onyechesi has written **"Keeping it Real"** as a gift to assist us all to see the joy in everyday life. He was born in Nigeria; studied Philosophy and Theology in Nigeria and was ordained a priest in August 2002. He has been a school principal,teacher and parish priest in Nigeria before he travelled to Belgium to further his studies in 2009. Fr Longinus arrived in Australia in 2011 and has worked in the parishes of Laverton, Altona Meadows, Noble Park, Keysborough, Heidelberg and has just been appointed Parish Administrator of Yea, and Alexandria.

His love of people, life, his smile and singing have brought much joy to the people he has met in his life's journey to date. Through his unique thoughtful writings we are invited to think and reflect on our own real life journey, see the joy and how we have been blessed.

His prayer is:
**"That God may give him the grace,
always and everywherc to make people happy"**